Nick Cave Biography

Songs of Love, Death, and Redemption

By
Edith A. Hall

Copyright © Edith A. Hall
2025 All rights reserved. No portion of this book may be reproduced in any form without written permission from the publisher or author, except as permitted by
U.S copyright law

Table of Contents

Chapter 1. Introduction

Chapter 2. Early Life and Artistic Foundations

Chapter 3. The Rise of The Bad Seeds

Chapter 4. Love and Obsession in His Music

Chapter 5. Dark Themes of Death and Violence

Chapter 6. Faith, Redemption, and the Search for Meaning

Chapter 7. Defining Albums and Their Impact

Chapter 8. Nick Cave as a Master Storyteller

Chapter 9. The Red Hand Files: A Window Into His Thoughts

Chapter 10. Cultural Impact and Legacy

11. Conclusion

Chapter 1. Introduction

Nick Cave is a singular figure in modern music and literature, an artist whose work transcends conventional genre boundaries and resonates with a profound emotional intensity. Over the past four decades, Cave has established himself as a master storyteller, blending poetry, music, and narrative into haunting compositions that explore love, death, violence, redemption, and the complexities of the human soul.

As the frontman of Nick Cave and the Bad Seeds, Cave has crafted a vast discography that oscillates between raw, furious energy and melancholic introspection. His early days with the post-punk outfit The Birthday Party showcased an unfiltered, anarchic aggression, but it was with the Bad Seeds that his songwriting matured into something uniquely powerful. With his deep, resonant voice, Cave delivers songs that feel almost literary—imbued with biblical imagery, gothic romance, and the unmistakable weight of personal experience.

Cave's impact extends beyond music. His novels, screenplays, and spoken-word performances further solidify his reputation as an artist of profound depth. His novels, And the Ass Saw the Angel (1989) and The Death of Bunny Munro (2009), reveal his affinity for Southern Gothic themes, while his contributions to films such as The Proposition (2005) and Lawless (2012) display his ability to translate his storytelling prowess into cinematic form.

Yet, what makes Cave a true "poet of darkness and emotion" is not just the breadth of his work, but the emotional authenticity with which he approaches his art. His music and writing are raw, deeply personal, and often unsettling, delving into the deepest corners of human suffering and salvation. His later albums, particularly Skeleton Tree (2016) and Ghosteen (2019), serve as deeply moving meditations on grief following the tragic death of his son, Arthur.

By examining Cave's lyrics, musical evolution, literary influences, and the impact of his personal life on his artistry, we can better understand why he remains one of the most profound and enduring figures in contemporary culture. This introduction will explore how Nick Cave has crafted a career built on storytelling, emotion, and an unwavering commitment to artistic truth.

Caves lyrics are often described as poetic, not only because of their richness in language but also due to their narrative depth and thematic complexity. Unlike many rock and alternative musicians, whose lyrics may serve as a backdrop to the music, Cave's words stand on their own, often resembling poems or short stories set to music.

From the early gothic ballads of From Her to Eternity (1984) to the introspective meditations on Ghosteen (2019), Cave's lyrics have remained deeply literary. His work is frequently infused with biblical allegory, drawing from Christian iconography to explore themes of sin, redemption, and divine justice. Songs like The Mercy Seat (1988), which tells the story of a man on death row, brim with religious overtones and existential weight, reflecting Cave's fascination with morality and fate.

Similarly, Red Right Hand (1994), perhaps one of his most well-known tracks, is a chilling, almost mythological tale of an enigmatic figure wielding power and judgment. The song's title is a reference to John Milton's Paradise Lost, reinforcing Cave's deep engagement with literary tradition. His use of dark, poetic imagery—"a shadow is cast wherever he stands, stacks of green paper in his red right hand"—paints an ominous picture that feels both timeless and eerily contemporary.

Beyond biblical and classical influences, Cave has often cited writers like William Faulkner, Flannery O'Connor, and Leonard Cohen as inspirations. The influence of Southern Gothic literature is particularly evident in his storytelling style, which often features deeply flawed characters, themes of decay and suffering, and an underlying sense of the supernatural.

Cave's career has been marked by a continuous evolution, both musically and thematically. His early work with The Birthday Party was defined by chaotic, almost nihilistic energy. Songs like Release the Bats and Junkyard were aggressive and discordant, showcasing a raw, unfiltered rage. However, even in these early years, Cave's lyrical style set him apart.

With the formation of Nick Cave and the Bad Seeds in 1983, his songwriting took on a more structured and narrative-driven approach. Albums such as The Firstborn Is Dead (1985) and Your Funeral... My Trial (1986) established his affinity for gothic storytelling, blending elements of blues, folk, and post-punk. His 1996 album Murder Ballads took this storytelling to its extreme, compiling a series of dark, often violent tales set to music.

Yet, while Cave has never shied away from exploring darkness, his later work has exhibited a shift towards vulnerability and introspection. The 2013 album Push the Sky Away marked a turning point, replacing bombastic arrangements with sparse, atmospheric compositions. This evolution was further amplified following the tragic death of his son Arthur in 2015, which profoundly influenced the deeply emotional albums Skeleton Tree and Ghosteen. These records abandoned conventional song structures in favor of ethereal, almost stream-of-consciousness lyrics, reflecting Cave's grief and search for meaning.

His ability to continually reinvent himself while maintaining a distinct artistic voice is a testament to his status as one of the most compelling musicians of his time.

One of the most defining aspects of Cave's recent work is his exploration of grief, particularly in response to the loss of his son. While his earlier music often dealt with death in an abstract or fictionalized manner, Skeleton Tree and Ghosteen are striking in their raw, personal emotion.

Songs like I Need You and Girl in Amber from Skeleton Tree capture the agony of loss with an almost unbearable intensity. The lyrics feel fragmented, as if Cave is grasping for meaning in the midst of sorrow. On Ghosteen, the themes of grief evolve into something more spiritual, with Cave portraying a sense of longing and hope for transcendence.

What makes Cave's approach to grief so compelling is his refusal to offer easy answers. His lyrics do not attempt to resolve pain but instead sit with it, allowing for both despair and moments of beauty. His openness about his grieving process, particularly through his Red Hand Files newsletter, has made his art even more resonant, offering a form of solace to those who have experienced similar loss.

Nick Cave's ability to channel profound emotion into his music and writing has made him an enduring and influential figure in contemporary culture. His work exists at the intersection of poetry, music, and storytelling, creating a body of work that is both deeply personal and universally resonant.

His influence can be seen in artists across genres, from alternative rock musicians to contemporary poets and filmmakers. His commitment to exploring the human experience—its suffering, its beauty, its contradictions—ensures that his work will continue to be relevant for generations to come.

Ultimately, Nick Cave is more than just a musician or a writer; he is a poet of darkness and emotion, an artist who confronts the deepest aspects of life with honesty and intensity. Whether through haunting ballads, gripping novels, or cinematic storytelling, Cave's work reminds us of the power of art to explore, heal, and transcend.

Chapter 2. Early Life and Artistic Foundations

Nicholas Edward Cave was born on September 22, 1957, in Warracknabeal, a small rural town in Victoria, Australia. He grew up in the nearby town of Wangaratta, surrounded by the stark Australian landscape that would later influence his storytelling and songwriting. His father, Colin Cave, was an English teacher and literary enthusiast, while his mother, Dawn Cave, worked as a librarian. This environment fostered a deep appreciation for literature and language from an early age.

Cave's father introduced him to the works of writers like Vladimir Nabokov, Fyodor Dostoevsky, and William Faulkner, shaping his fascination with dark, poetic storytelling. The tragic and the gothic were ever-present themes in the books he read, foreshadowing the lyrical depth and narrative complexity that would define his later work.

Despite his literary leanings, Cave's early life was also marked by rebellion. He attended Caulfield Grammar School in Melbourne, where he was known as an intelligent but unruly student. His love for art led him to enroll at the Caulfield Institute of Technology to study painting, but music ultimately became his true passion. It was during this period that he immersed himself in the burgeoning punk and post-punk scenes, seeking an outlet for his creative energy and emotional intensity.

A pivotal moment in Cave's life occurred when his father died in a car accident in 1978. The loss deeply affected him, intensifying the themes of grief, religion, and mortality that would echo throughout his career. This tragedy fueled his artistic drive, pushing him further into music and poetry as a means of expressing the depth of his emotions.

The Birth of The Birthday Party and Punk Roots

Nick Cave's first significant step into the music world came with the formation of The Boys Next Door in the mid-1970s. The band, which he formed with friends from Caulfield Grammar, including Mick Harvey, Tracy Pew, and Phill Calvert, initially played a mix of punk and post-punk music. Their early sound was influenced by artists such as David Bowie, The Stooges, and Lou Reed.

By 1978, the band had gained a cult following in Australia's underground scene. However, feeling constrained by the limitations of their homeland, they relocated to London in 1980, renaming themselves The Birthday Party. This transformation marked a dramatic shift in their musical style—embracing a chaotic, aggressive energy that fused punk with avant-garde noise and dark, theatrical lyrics.

The Birthday Party quickly developed a reputation for their volatile live performances. Cave, as the band's frontman, delivered raw, almost violent performances, often writhing on stage and screaming lyrics that bordered on the macabre. Their music was heavily influenced by the bleak poetry of the Beat Generation, German Expressionism, and American blues, all of which added to their unique sound.

They released a series of albums, including Prayers on Fire (1981) and Junkyard (1982), which solidified their reputation as one of the most innovative and anarchic bands of the post-punk movement. However, internal tensions, drug abuse, and Cave's increasingly dominant artistic vision led to the band's disbandment in 1983.

Despite their relatively short lifespan, The Birthday Party laid the foundation for Cave's future musical explorations. Their fusion of punk aggression with literary lyricism set the stage for his evolution into one of the most distinctive songwriters of his generation.

Literary and Musical Influences

Cave's artistic influences were as varied as they were profound. His love for literature, instilled by his father, played a crucial role in shaping his songwriting. He was particularly drawn to the works of William Blake, whose fusion of poetry and spirituality resonated deeply with him. Similarly, the existential weight of Dostoevsky and the Southern Gothic darkness of Flannery O'Connor found their way into his lyrics.

Musically, Cave's early inspirations included the raw energy of punk bands like The Stooges and The Ramones, as well as the dark, storytelling tradition of Johnny Cash and Leonard Cohen. The latter two artists, known for their deeply poetic lyrics and brooding vocal styles, had a lasting impact on Cave's approach to songwriting.

Blues music was another major influence. Cave was fascinated by the haunting quality of Delta blues, particularly artists like Robert Johnson and Skip James. The themes of sin, redemption, and suffering found in blues music aligned perfectly with his own artistic obsessions.

His interest in religious imagery—despite being an avowed atheist in his early years—also shaped his songwriting. Biblical references and themes of faith, guilt, and salvation became recurring motifs in his work, often adding a sense of grand, mythic drama to his lyrics.

As he moved beyond The Birthday Party, Cave refined his literary approach to songwriting. He embraced a more narrative-driven style, creating characters and stories that felt like gothic short stories set to music. His ability to blend poetic lyricism with raw emotional intensity made him one of the most distinctive voices in alternative music.

The foundation laid in these early years—his literary upbringing, punk roots, and diverse artistic influences—would propel Nick Cave into a career that would span decades, evolving from punk provocateur to one of the most revered songwriters and storytellers of his generation.

Chapter 3. The Rise of The Bad Seeds

Nick Cave's journey from the raw, chaotic energy of The Birthday Party to the poetic and sophisticated artistry of The Bad Seeds is a testament to his evolution as an artist. While The Birthday Party was marked by destructive performances and nihilistic themes, Cave's transition to The Bad Seeds signified a deeper engagement with narrative songwriting, musical diversity, and emotional depth.

After The Birthday Party disbanded in 1983, Cave and Mick Harvey sought a new direction—one that retained the ferocity of their punk roots but allowed for greater experimentation. Their vision materialized with the formation of Nick Cave & The Bad Seeds, a band that would become one of the most influential alternative rock groups of all time.

Cave's artistic brilliance emerged from chaos, shaped by personal struggles, an insatiable literary appetite, and a fascination with biblical imagery, romance, and mortality. In the early days, his songwriting was still raw and aggressive, but by the late 1980s and early 1990s, he had honed a distinct storytelling style, blending myth, folklore, and personal anguish into deeply moving compositions.

The transformation was evident in albums like Tender Prey (1988), featuring the haunting "The Mercy Seat," a song about a condemned man facing execution. Cave's ability to balance brutality with tenderness became a defining characteristic of his music. The intensity of his live performances also shifted; while his stage presence remained magnetic, it became more controlled and theatrical, enhancing the dramatic impact of his lyrics.

Throughout the decades, Cave faced periods of addiction and personal turmoil, but these struggles often fueled his artistic reinvention. His move toward piano-based ballads and introspective storytelling in the mid-1990s marked another turning point, culminating in the critically acclaimed The Boatman's Call (1997), a deeply personal and melancholic album inspired by heartbreak and spiritual reflection.

Evolution of the Band and Key Collaborations

Nick Cave & The Bad Seeds were never a static entity. The band's lineup evolved over the years, each change bringing fresh dynamics and influences to their sound.

The Early Years: Establishing the Band's Identity

When The Bad Seeds were formed, Cave brought together an eclectic group of musicians, including Mick Harvey (multi-instrumentalist and longtime collaborator), Blixa Bargeld (guitarist from Einstürzende Neubauten), Barry Adamson (bassist from Magazine), and Hugo Race. Their debut album, From Her to Eternity (1984), set the stage for what was to come—a blend of gothic rock, blues, and post-punk intensity.

Bargeld's abrasive guitar work played a crucial role in defining the band's early sound, particularly on albums like The Firstborn Is Dead (1985) and Your Funeral... My Trial (1986). His departure in 2003 marked a significant shift in the band's sonic identity.

The Warren Ellis Era: A New Soundscape

One of the most significant collaborations in Cave's career has been with violinist and multi-instrumentalist Warren Ellis. Ellis, who joined The Bad Seeds in the mid-1990s, gradually became

Cave's most trusted musical partner. His influence was particularly notable in Push the Sky Away (2013) and Skeleton Tree (2016), where atmospheric soundscapes and minimalist arrangements replaced the raw aggression of earlier albums.

Ellis's contributions extended beyond The Bad Seeds. The duo's work on film scores, including The Proposition (2005), The Road (2009), and Wind River (2017), showcased their ability to create haunting, cinematic compositions. Their deep musical bond led to the formation of Grinderman, a side project that revived Cave's wilder, more aggressive tendencies in the mid-2000s.

Collaborations with Other Artists

Nick Cave has collaborated with a wide range of artists, each partnership adding another layer to his artistic legacy.

PJ Harvey: Cave's brief but intense romantic and musical relationship with PJ Harvey resulted in the haunting duet "Henry Lee" (1996). Their chemistry was palpable, both in the song and in their evocative music video.

Kylie Minogue: Perhaps his most unexpected collaboration, Cave's duet with Kylie Minogue on "Where the Wild Roses Grow" (1995) was a defining moment in his career. The song's dark, tragic narrative paired with Minogue's ethereal vocals introduced Cave to a wider audience.

Johnny Cash: Cave's admiration for Johnny Cash was mutual. Cash covered Cave's song "The Mercy Seat," a testament to its powerful storytelling.

Cave's collaborations have always been about pushing boundaries, merging genres, and exploring the depths of human emotion. Whether working with fellow rock musicians, orchestral composers, or film directors, he consistently brings a unique and poetic sensibility to his projects.

Crafting a Unique Sound

The sound of Nick Cave & The Bad Seeds is difficult to categorize. Over the years, it has encompassed gothic rock, blues, post-punk, orchestral arrangements, and electronic elements. The band's willingness to evolve and experiment has kept their music fresh and relevant across decades.

Early Rawness and Post-Punk Energy

In the early years, The Bad Seeds built upon the chaotic energy of The Birthday Party, but with a greater focus on structured songwriting. From Her to Eternity (1984) featured a mix of brooding ballads and explosive outbursts, setting the template for Cave's later work. The Firstborn Is Dead (1985) leaned into blues influences, drawing inspiration from American Southern Gothic themes and legends like Elvis Presley.

The Dark Storytelling Period

By the late 1980s and early 1990s, Cave had embraced a more literary approach to songwriting. Albums like Tender Prey (1988) and The Good Son (1990) balanced violence with beauty, using religious imagery and poetic storytelling. Henry's Dream (1992) and Let Love In (1994) continued this tradition, featuring songs that blended love, murder, and redemption.

The Piano Ballad Era

Cave's shift toward piano-based ballads marked a new artistic phase. The Boatman's Call (1997) was a departure from the band's earlier, more aggressive work. Songs like "Into My Arms" and "People Ain't No Good" were stripped-down and deeply personal, showcasing Cave's ability to convey raw emotion with minimal instrumentation.

Experimental and Ambient Exploration

The 2000s and 2010s saw The Bad Seeds experimenting with new sounds. Push the Sky Away (2013) introduced electronic textures and atmospheric production, moving away from traditional rock instrumentation. Skeleton Tree (2016) and Ghosteen (2019) were deeply influenced by personal tragedy, particularly the loss of Cave's son, Arthur. These albums embraced ambient elements, spoken word, and ethereal soundscapes, marking a new level of emotional depth in Cave's music.

The Influence of Film Scores

Cave and Warren Ellis's work on film soundtracks has also shaped The Bad Seeds' evolving sound. Their minimalist, haunting compositions for films like The Assassination of Jesse James by the Coward Robert Ford (2007) and Hell or High Water (2016) introduced new atmospheric and cinematic elements into their studio albums.

Enduring Legacy and Continued Reinvention

Even after decades in the industry, Cave continues to reinvent himself. His ability to blend storytelling, music, and raw emotion has ensured that The Bad Seeds remain relevant, influencing countless artists across multiple genres. From punk origins to orchestral grandeur, from love songs to murder ballads, Cave's artistry is defined by an unwavering commitment to evolution and authenticity.

As The Bad Seeds continue to push boundaries, Nick Cave's journey remains a testament to the power of artistic transformation. Whether through chaos, heartbreak, or reinvention, he has crafted a musical legacy that transcends generations.

Chapter 4. Love and Obsession in His Music

Nick Cave's music is often defined by its deep emotional intensity, where love is rarely straightforward or simple. Instead, it manifests as an all-consuming force, entwined with obsession, violence, tragedy, and longing. His lyrics explore love not just as a tender sentiment but as an overwhelming, often destructive power. Across his work with The Birthday Party, The Bad Seeds, and Grinderman, Cave has repeatedly dissected the complexities of human desire, painting love as both an ecstatic and ruinous experience.

From the raw, chaotic energy of his early work to the refined storytelling of his later albums, love and obsession have remained constant themes. Whether depicting a passionate, doomed affair in The Boatman's Call or delving into Biblical and mythical influences in Murder Ballads, Cave's songwriting captures the duality of love—both its beauty and its brutality. The violence of obsession is particularly evident in songs like "Where the Wild Roses Grow", where love and death are inseparable.

In Cave's world, love often leads to destruction, but it is also a source of redemption. His album Push the Sky Away explores a more ethereal, haunting form of devotion, with tracks like "Jubilee Street" illustrating love's ability to consume and transform. Similarly, Ghosteen shifts his focus toward transcendental love, reflecting his personal grief and longing.

Passion, Romance, and Devotion in His Lyrics

Nick Cave's lyricism is rooted in a deep literary tradition, blending poetry, Gothic romance, and biblical allegory. His songs about love are rarely simple ballads; they are often fraught with intensity and devotion bordering on madness. Throughout his career, Cave has channeled his fascination with grand, tragic love stories, drawing inspiration from writers such as Vladimir Nabokov, Leonard Cohen, and William Blake.

One of his most deeply romantic albums, The Boatman's Call, marks a departure from his earlier violent, theatrical love songs. Instead, it presents an introspective, confessional form of songwriting, where Cave lays bare his emotions with raw vulnerability. Songs like "Into My Arms" and "Far from Me" reflect on the pain of lost love and the unwavering devotion that lingers even after separation.

His fascination with biblical imagery often amplifies the sense of devotion in his lyrics. Songs like "Brompton Oratory" turn religious longing into a metaphor for romantic yearning, blurring the lines between sacred and profane love. This intertwining of passion and spiritual devotion is a recurring theme in Cave's songwriting, where love becomes almost a divine force—both a blessing and a curse.

Even in his later years, Cave continues to explore love with the same fervor but with a greater sense of reflection. Skeleton Tree and Ghosteen move beyond romantic passion to explore love's endurance in the face of loss. Songs like "Girl in Amber" and "Waiting for You" reflect the agony of grief, where love persists even when the object of affection is gone.

Songs of Longing and Heartache

Cave's discography is filled with songs that capture the ache of unfulfilled love. His ability to articulate longing has made many of his compositions deeply resonant, often depicting characters who are consumed by their desires.

In tracks like "The Weeping Song", Cave channels the universal sorrow of love lost, turning it into a dramatic, almost theatrical lament. His ability to convey emotional pain is particularly powerful in "Are You the One That I've Been Waiting For?", where he expresses a deep yearning for a love that remains just out of reach.

Heartache in Cave's music is not just about lost romance but also about existential sorrow. On Skeleton Tree, which was shaped by personal tragedy, songs like "I Need You" become desperate pleas for connection, capturing the raw pain of longing for someone who is absent. This album, along with Ghosteen, represents some of the most profound explorations of heartache in Cave's career, marking a shift from romantic despair to a broader meditation on loss and the persistence of love beyond death.

Even in his most aggressive, violent narratives, longing plays a crucial role. In Murder Ballads, the obsession that fuels the crimes is often rooted in a desperate, misguided longing. "The Kindness of Strangers" and "Henry Lee" depict love as something that leads to tragedy, reinforcing the idea that desire, when left unchecked, can turn destructive.

Personal Relationships Shaping His Art

Cave's personal relationships have played a significant role in shaping his music. His highly publicized relationship with PJ Harvey, for instance, deeply influenced The Boatman's Call. The breakup between the two artists led to some of Cave's most introspective and heart-wrenching lyrics, with many songs speculated to be directly inspired by their relationship.

Similarly, his deep love for his wife, Susie Bick, has been a major influence on his later work. Songs like "Breathless" from Abattoir Blues/The Lyre of Orpheus celebrate love with an uncharacteristic lightness, reflecting the joy and stability she brought into his life. However, tragedy has also played a significant role in his songwriting. The death of his son, Arthur, in 2015 profoundly shaped Skeleton Tree and Ghosteen, where love and grief are inextricably linked.

Cave's ability to channel his personal experiences into universal themes of love, obsession, and longing has cemented his reputation as one of the most powerful songwriters of his generation. Whether portraying love as a force of destruction, devotion, or salvation, his music continues to captivate audiences with its emotional depth and poetic brilliance.

Chapter 5. Dark Themes of Death and Violence

Nick Cave has long been fascinated by themes of death, violence, and the darker aspects of human nature. His lyrics often depict murder, revenge, and moral decay, blending them with poetic storytelling and visceral imagery. This preoccupation with mortality and brutality can be traced back to his deep literary influences, including the gothic horror of Edgar Allan Poe, the biblical narratives of punishment and redemption, and the existential despair found in Dostoevsky's work.

From his early days with The Birthday Party, Cave's music was steeped in chaotic, almost violent energy. Songs like Release the Bats and Big Jesus Trash Can displayed a raw, nihilistic edge that reflected the bands punk and post-punk influences. The aggression in his music wasn't just for show—it was an expression of his inner turmoil, his struggles with addiction, and his search for meaning in a world filled with suffering.

However, it was with The Bad Seeds that Cave refined this darkness into something more sophisticated and haunting. Tracks such as The Carny (from Your Funeral... My Trial, 1986) and The Mercy Seat (from Tender Prey, 1988) exemplify his ability to weave tales of crime, punishment, and existential dread. The Mercy Seat, in particular, is one of Cave's most chilling narratives, told from the perspective of a death-row inmate awaiting execution. The songs relentless, looping structure mirrors the character's fevered mind, building tension and emotional weight with each repetition.

The way Cave approaches death and violence in his music is not purely gratuitous; rather, he explores them as metaphysical concepts. He dissects the human condition through the lens of brutality, examining the consequences of violence and the moral ambiguity surrounding it. Unlike many artists who romanticize crime and rebellion, Cave presents violence as something primal and inescapable, often rooted in passion, obsession, or divine reckoning.

Murder Ballads and Gothic Narratives

If there's one album that fully encapsulates Nick Cave's obsession with violence, it's Murder Ballads (1996). This collection of traditional and original murder ballads is an exploration of storytelling, crime, and the macabre. The album contains some of Cave's most unsettling songs, blending folk traditions with his signature dark poeticism.

The opening track, Song of Joy, sets the tone with a narrator who recounts the gruesome murder of his wife and children in a disturbingly detached manner. The ambiguity of whether he is the murderer himself adds a layer of psychological horror. This method of storytelling—where the truth is obscured, and the unreliable narrator leaves room for interpretation—became a hallmark of Cave's songwriting.

Perhaps the most infamous song on the album is Stagger Lee, a reinterpretation of a traditional folk song about a ruthless outlaw. Cave's version amplifies the violence and depravity to an almost surreal degree, turning Stagger Lee into a sadistic, unstoppable force. The graphic nature of the lyrics sparked controversy, but Cave defended the song as a reflection of folklore's raw and unfiltered storytelling traditions.

Murder Ballads also features Where the Wild Roses Grow, a duet with Kylie Minogue that became one of Cave's biggest commercial successes. The song tells the story of a man who kills his lover, justifying it as an act of devotion. The contrast between Minogue's delicate, innocent vocals and Cave's sinister delivery makes the song even more haunting. The tracks success demonstrated that Cave's gothic storytelling could resonate with a mainstream audience without losing its eerie allure.

Beyond Murder Ballads, Cave has continued to explore gothic narratives in his work. Songs like Red Right Hand (from Let Love In, 1994) introduce shadowy figures of power and menace, evoking imagery of both the devil and corrupt authority figures. The song's mysterious antagonist, wielding an unseen influence, has been widely interpreted as a metaphor for fate, government control, or even the devil himself.

Cave's ability to craft intricate gothic stories stems from his literary influences. The southern gothic works of Flannery O'Connor, the bleak existentialism of Cormac McCarthy, and the haunting poetry of Leonard Cohen all play a role in shaping his lyrical world. His narratives are rarely straightforward; they are layered with symbolism, unreliable narrators, and moral dilemmas, making them feel like timeless myths rather than simple songs.

Religious Symbolism and Moral Struggles

One of the most distinctive aspects of Nick Cave's work is his deep engagement with religious themes. While he has described himself as being more spiritual than traditionally religious, his lyrics are rich with biblical imagery, questions of faith, and struggles with morality.

Cave's fascination with the Bible is not that of a devout believer but rather that of an artist wrestling with its themes. He often portrays God as an ambiguous or even indifferent force, and his characters frequently grapple with sin, redemption, and divine justice. Songs like The Mercy Seat and The Witness Song (from The Good Son, 1990) play with these ideas, blurring the lines between religious salvation and damnation.

One of his most profound religious explorations comes in Abattoir Blues / The Lyre of Orpheus (2004). The album juxtaposes biblical grandeur with human frailty, as seen in There She Goes, My Beautiful World, where Cave sings of literary figures struggling for divine inspiration. The title track, The Lyre of Orpheus, retells the Greek myth of Orpheus but infuses it with a brutal, irreverent twist, portraying Orpheus as a careless creator whose actions lead to destruction.

Cave's relationship with religion became even more pronounced in his later work, particularly after the tragic death of his son, Arthur, in 2015. Albums like Skeleton Tree (2016) and Ghosteen (2019) see Cave grappling with grief, searching for meaning in loss, and questioning the nature of existence. Ghosteen, in particular, is filled with ethereal, almost hymn-like compositions that reflect a man both shattered by and in awe of the mysteries of life and death.

In his Red Hand Files letters—an online platform where Cave answers fan questions—he has spoken about how his faith has evolved over time. He describes a form of belief that is less about doctrine and more about love, connection, and the transformative power of grief. His religious imagery, then, is not about strict adherence to dogma but about using ancient symbols to make sense of human suffering.

Finding Beauty in Tragedy

For all the darkness in his music, Nick Cave is ultimately an artist who finds beauty in tragedy. His songs, while often filled with sorrow and violence, are deeply poetic and emotionally resonant. He does not shy away from pain; rather, he transforms it into something profound and transcendent.

This aspect of his artistry became especially evident after the personal loss he suffered in 2015. Skeleton Tree and Ghosteen marked a shift in his songwriting—moving away from the narrative-driven gothic tales of his earlier work to a more abstract, meditative style. Songs like I Need You and Bright Horses ache with raw vulnerability, reflecting a man who has been broken but who still finds solace in love, memory, and artistic expression.

Cave's ability to extract beauty from pain is one of the reasons his work continues to resonate with audiences. His music acknowledges suffering but also suggests that through art, connection, and storytelling, we can find a sense of meaning. Even in his darkest songs, there is a poetic elegance—a reminder that despair and beauty often exist side by side.

His performances, too, reflect this emotional depth. Whether delivering an intense, almost preacher-like sermon on stage or sitting at a piano pouring his heart into a delicate ballad, Cave's presence is hypnotic. His work speaks to something primal and universal: the need to confront darkness, to tell stories, and to find moments of grace amid the chaos.

Nick Cave's music is an unflinching journey through the darkest corners of the human experience. He explores death and violence not as mere shock value but as fundamental elements of storytelling. His murder ballads and gothic narratives capture the terror and beauty of life's fragility, while his use of religious symbolism reveals a deep and evolving moral struggle. Yet, for all the darkness, Cave's art is ultimately about transcendence—about finding beauty, even in sorrow.

His legacy is one of poetic intensity, fearless exploration, and unwavering emotional honesty. In every song, every story, and every whispered lyric, Cave reminds us that art has the power to confront our deepest fears and, in doing so, bring us closer to understanding what it means to be human.

Chapter 6. Faith, Redemption, and the Search for Meaning

Nick Cave's music and writing are steeped in themes of faith and redemption, exploring the complexities of human existence through the lens of spirituality, sin, and salvation. His work often delves into the tension between divine grace and human fallibility, drawing from personal experiences, literature, and biblical narratives to create a body of work that is both deeply personal and universally resonant.

Cave's fascination with faith is not rooted in strict religious doctrine but rather in an existential quest for meaning. His lyrics frequently depict characters struggling with guilt, seeking redemption, or grappling with the consequences of their actions. Albums like The Firstborn Is Dead (1985), Tender Prey (1988), and The Boatman's Call (1997) illustrate this ongoing exploration of moral reckoning and the possibility of redemption.

Songs such as "The Mercy Seat" epitomize Cave's meditations on judgment and grace. The track, written from the perspective of a condemned man awaiting execution, is rich with religious imagery, drawing parallels between the electric chair and Christ's crucifixion. The song's protagonist swings between defiance and remorse, reflecting Cave's broader thematic concerns: Is redemption possible for even the most broken souls? Does faith provide salvation, or is it merely a construct we cling to in times of despair?

Cave's search for meaning is also evident in his personal life. His engagement with faith has evolved over time, shaped by personal tragedies, philosophical inquiries, and artistic pursuits. Rather than providing definitive answers, his work embraces the contradictions inherent in spirituality, presenting faith as a complex, ever-shifting force rather than a rigid doctrine.

Biblical Imagery and Spiritual Undertones

Biblical allusions are a defining feature of Cave's songwriting, lending his work a sense of grandeur and timelessness. His lyrics are often populated by Old Testament prophets, vengeful gods, sinners, and saints, creating a mythic atmosphere that underscores the emotional intensity of his music.

From the early years of The Birthday Party to his later work with The Bad Seeds, Cave has drawn upon biblical narratives to frame his songs. Tracks such as "Tupelo" reimagine the birth of Elvis Presley as an apocalyptic event, mirroring the biblical flood and the coming of a messianic figure. Similarly, "Red Right Hand" presents a dark, omniscient force reminiscent of God's hand of justice in the Book of Exodus, adding a layer of foreboding to the song's gothic storytelling.

Albums like Tender Prey and Let Love In (1994) showcase Cave's ability to weave scriptural references into modern narratives of love, violence, and redemption. "Do You Love Me?" carries echoes of the Song of Solomon, while "Up Jumped the Devil" channels the devilish trickery of Job's adversary. These biblical influences enrich Cave's work, elevating his songs beyond mere storytelling into the realm of myth and allegory.

Beyond direct biblical references, Cave's music exudes a spiritual undertone that speaks to the human longing for transcendence. His compositions often carry the weight of religious hymns, with solemn organ chords, gospel choirs, and poetic lyricism that evoke the sacred. Whether singing of damnation or deliverance, Cave's use of biblical imagery underscores the spiritual stakes of his narratives, lending them a depth that resonates across cultures and belief systems.

Wrestling with Belief and Doubt

Cave's relationship with faith is anything but static. His career is marked by a continuous struggle between belief and skepticism, a push-and-pull dynamic that infuses his music with urgency and depth. Unlike artists who adopt a fixed religious stance, Cave embraces the ambiguity of faith, allowing his work to reflect the complexities of spiritual yearning and existential doubt.

Throughout his discography, Cave's lyrics oscillate between reverence and irreverence. Some songs present faith as a source of solace, while others depict it as an unattainable or even oppressive force. On The Boatman's Call, Cave moves away from the fire-and-brimstone intensity of earlier works, adopting a more introspective and contemplative tone. Songs like "Into My Arms" reject a conventional notion of God while still expressing a deep spiritual longing, illustrating the paradox of belief in an age of skepticism.

Cave's writing also explores the struggle of reconciling faith with suffering. The tragic loss of his son, Arthur, in 2015 profoundly impacted his artistic perspective, deepening his engagement with questions of grief, existence, and the divine. Albums like Skeleton Tree (2016) and Ghosteen (2019) reflect this period of mourning, presenting faith not as an easy answer but as a fragile, flickering light in the darkness.

In interviews and his Red Hand Files letters, Cave has spoken candidly about his evolving relationship with faith. He acknowledges that while he may not adhere to traditional religious beliefs, he finds value in the concept of the sacred, in art, love, and human connection. This openness to uncertainty defines his artistic philosophy, allowing him to explore faith not as a dogma but as an ongoing dialogue between doubt and belief.

The Tension Between Hope and Despair

Cave's music exists in the liminal space between hope and despair, capturing the fragile balance between the two. His songs often depict characters standing at the crossroads of ruin and redemption, their fates hinging on a moment of grace or destruction. This duality—between light and darkness, salvation and damnation—lies at the heart of his artistic vision.

Hope, in Cave's work, is often hard-won. It is not a naive optimism but a defiant assertion in the face of suffering. Tracks like "Push the Sky Away" embody this quiet resilience, urging the listener to keep moving forward despite uncertainty. Similarly, Ghosteen presents a vision of grief that, while devastating, ultimately embraces the possibility of healing and transcendence.

At the same time, despair is an ever-present force in Cave's work. Albums like Murder Ballads (1996) revel in narratives of doom, while Skeleton Tree is a raw expression of loss and mourning. Yet, even in the darkest moments, Cave's music rarely succumbs to nihilism. Instead, it acknowledges pain while seeking something beyond it—a glimpse of beauty, a flicker of faith, a reason to continue.

This tension between despair and hope is what makes Cave's work so compelling. His songs do not offer easy resolutions; instead, they embrace the complexities of human existence, reflecting the contradictions of faith, love, and grief. Whether through biblical allegories, haunting ballads, or existential musings, Cave crafts a world in which the sacred and the profane coexist, where redemption is always possible but never guaranteed.

Cave's exploration of faith, redemption, and existential longing has cemented his place as one of the most profound songwriters of his generation. His work does not seek to provide answers but instead invites the listener into a dialogue—one that acknowledges the beauty and terror of existence, the flickering nature of belief, and the enduring search for meaning in an uncertain world.

Chapter 7. Defining Albums and Their Impact

Nick Cave's career has been marked by a restless creative spirit and an unyielding commitment to storytelling. Across multiple decades, his albums have not only defined his evolution as an artist but have also left an indelible mark on alternative music. Whether embracing the raw energy of post-punk, the chilling narratives of gothic blues, or the tender reflections of love and loss, Cave's work showcases his mastery of songcraft. Among his many records, five albums stand out as pivotal in shaping both his artistry and his audience's perception of his work.

The Firstborn Is Dead: Blues and Southern Gothic Influences (1985)

After the disintegration of The Birthday Party, Cave and his new band, The Bad Seeds, set out to carve a unique sound that drew from deep musical traditions. The Firstborn Is Dead, the band's second studio album, established their commitment to blending rock, blues, and literary ambition. The album, named after a line in a biography of Elvis

Presley, taps into the American South's mythos, despite Cave being an outsider to its geography.

Sonically, The Firstborn Is Dead is a raw, stripped-down exploration of blues, infused with the dark, violent energy that had defined Cave's previous work. The album opens with "Tupelo," a stormy, apocalyptic reimagining of Presley's birth in a rain-drenched Mississippi town. With relentless drumming, menacing basslines, and Cave's commanding vocals, the song sets the tone for an album steeped in gothic storytelling. The track's layered imagery, featuring biblical floods and prophetic visions, cements Cave's fascination with myth-making.

Another standout track, "Knockin' on Joe," is a stark, slow-burning piece that presents a bleak vision of imprisonment. The song's droning, hypnotic quality and minimalist instrumentation reflect the agony of being trapped in both a literal and metaphorical sense. Similarly, "Wanted Man," a Johnny Cash song reworked with Cave's lyrical additions, bridges traditional outlaw folklore with Cave's signature lyrical flourishes.

By immersing himself in blues and Southern Gothic influences, Cave channeled the themes of sin, redemption, and violence that would define much of his later work. The Firstborn Is Dead marked a crucial turning point, proving that Cave was more than just a post-punk provocateur—he was a storyteller with a deep understanding of musical and literary traditions.

Tender Prey: Establishing an Iconic Sound (1988)

With Tender Prey, Cave refined his sonic identity, crafting an album that captured the rawness of his earlier years while hinting at the sophistication to come. The album's standout track, "The Mercy Seat," remains one of his most iconic songs, a relentless, harrowing account of a condemned man awaiting execution. The song's circular structure, urgent instrumentation, and feverish delivery make it a masterclass in dramatic tension. Its themes of guilt, redemption, and the blurred line between justice and vengeance encapsulate Cave's ongoing preoccupations.

Beyond "The Mercy Seat," Tender Prey explores a range of moods and styles. "Up Jumped the Devil" embraces a sinister, theatrical energy, featuring Cave's vivid storytelling and devilish charm. "Deanna" offers a frenzied, almost rockabilly-inspired murder ballad, blending violence with dark humor. In contrast, "Slowly Goes the Night" reveals Cave's growing ability to craft deeply emotional ballads, foreshadowing his later work.

Lyrically, the album is drenched in religious imagery, desperation, and fatalism, mirroring Cave's personal struggles during this period. His battles with addiction and self-destruction seep into the lyrics, lending the songs a raw, confessional quality. Tender Prey solidified Cave's reputation as a master of macabre storytelling and established many of the themes that would continue to define his work.

Murder Ballads: Tales of Crime and Consequence (1996)

While violence and crime had long been present in Cave's work, Murder Ballads took these elements to their extreme. A concept album built entirely around tales of murder and mayhem, it revels in its blood-soaked narratives while also exploring the emotional and moral weight of such stories.

The album's most famous track, "Where the Wild Roses Grow," featuring Kylie Minogue, became an unexpected mainstream success. The song's haunting duet presents a chilling, poetic take on a murder ballad, where beauty and brutality intertwine. Minogue's delicate vocals contrast with Cave's dark, ominous delivery, making it one of his most commercially accessible yet thematically disturbing songs.

Other tracks, such as "Stagger Lee" and "The Curse of Millhaven," embrace over-the-top violence with a sense of theatricality. "Stagger Lee" reinterprets the traditional folk song, amplifying its brutality with grotesque imagery and an unrelenting, bluesy groove. Meanwhile, "The Curse of Millhaven" is a gleefully macabre tale of a young girl who murders for pleasure, narrated with a manic energy.

Yet, Murder Ballads is not just about shock value—it is also a meditation on storytelling itself. By drawing from folk traditions and infusing them with his own narrative voice, Cave explores the nature of violence in art and history. The album cemented his reputation as a master of dark, literary songwriting and introduced his work to a wider audience.

The Boatman's Call: Introspective and Heartfelt Lyricism (1997)

Following the theatrical carnage of Murder Ballads, Cave took a sharp turn inward with The Boatman's

Call. This album is one of his most intimate and deeply personal works, stripping away much of the bombast in favor of sparse, piano-driven arrangements.

Many of the songs on The Boatman's Call were influenced by Cave's personal relationships, particularly his romances with PJ Harvey and Brazilian journalist Viviane Carneiro. Tracks like "Into My Arms" and "West Country Girl" carry a tenderness that feels almost vulnerable compared to his previous work. "Into My Arms" is especially notable for its simplicity and emotional rawness, expressing both love and a quiet crisis of faith.

Lyrically, the album is filled with themes of love, loss, and spiritual searching. "People Ain't No Good" is a melancholic meditation on human nature, while "Brompton Oratory" blends romantic longing with religious imagery. Cave's fascination with faith continues here, but instead of the fire-and-brimstone intensity of earlier albums, The Boatman's Call presents a quieter, more contemplative spirituality.

This album marked a significant transformation in Cave's artistic trajectory. It proved that he could be just as compelling when baring his soul as when crafting dark, elaborate narratives. The raw honesty of The Boatman's Call resonated with fans and critics alike, solidifying it as one of his most beloved works.

Ghosteen: Grief, Loss, and Transformation (2019)

More than two decades after The Boatman's Call, Cave released Ghosteen, an album born from unimaginable grief. Following the tragic death of his son Arthur in 2015, Cave's songwriting took on a new depth of sorrow and introspection. Unlike previous albums, where death and loss were explored through fictional narratives, Ghosteen is deeply personal, a meditation on mourning, love, and transcendence.

The album's two-part structure divides it into "children" and "parents," symbolizing different stages of grief. Songs like "Bright Horses" and "Waiting for You" carry an aching, dreamlike quality, where hope and despair exist side by side. The lyrics are poetic, abstract, and filled with ghostly imagery, creating a sense of spiritual liminality.

Musically, Ghosteen is ethereal and atmospheric, relying more on synths and ambient textures than the band's traditional rock elements. Warren Ellis's contributions play a significant role in shaping the album's sound, adding layers of delicate beauty to Cave's haunting vocals.

What makes Ghosteen so powerful is its ability to turn grief into something transcendent. It is not just an album about loss but also about transformation, acceptance, and the search for meaning in suffering. With Ghosteen, Cave delivered one of his most profoundly moving works, reaffirming his status as one of the greatest songwriters of his generation.

Throughout his career, Nick Cave has continually evolved, never content to stay in one artistic space for too long. Each of these defining albums represents a different facet of his creative journey—from the dark Southern blues of The Firstborn Is Dead to the haunting grief of Ghosteen. Together, they form a body of work that is both deeply personal and universally resonant, ensuring Cave's legacy as a musician, poet, and storyteller of the highest order.

Chapter 8. Nick Cave as a Master Storyteller

Nick Cave's artistic career has been defined by his mastery of storytelling, a trait that transcends his music and seeps into literature, screenwriting, and poetic narratives. His ability to craft intricate, deeply evocative tales has solidified him as one of the most compelling storytellers of his generation. Whether through the dark, Gothic ballads of The Bad Seeds, his novels that explore existential themes, or his ventures into screenwriting, Cave's storytelling remains haunting, poetic, and unflinchingly honest.

Nick Cave as a Master Storyteller

Nick Cave's songs are not mere compositions; they are narratives, rich with detail, emotion, and thematic complexity. His ability to weave gripping stories into his music sets him apart from many of his contemporaries. Throughout his career, he has drawn from literature, history, folklore, and personal experience, blending them into compelling and immersive songs.

Dark Narratives and Morality Tales

One of Cave's defining storytelling techniques is his use of dark, often violent narratives. Songs like Stagger Lee from Murder Ballads (1996) are prime examples of how he reinterprets folk tales and traditional ballads, amplifying their brutality and adding layers of psychological depth. He often explores themes of crime, vengeance, and morality, painting vivid pictures of outlaws, sinners, and lost souls.

His ability to inhabit the minds of flawed characters —killers, preachers, lovers, and ghosts—creates a cinematic quality in his music. A song like The Mercy Seat (1988), which tells the story of a man facing execution, showcases Cave's talent for immersing the listener in a character's psyche. The song's protagonist, condemned and defiant, experiences a mix of guilt, fear, and religious conviction, making for an intense and harrowing narrative.

Emotional Depth and Human Struggles

Beyond the dark and violent themes, Cave also explores themes of love, longing, and human frailty. His ballads, such as Into My Arms and Love Letter, demonstrate a softer yet equally powerful side of his storytelling. These songs are deeply poetic, tapping into themes of devotion, heartbreak, and spiritual yearning. His lyricism in these pieces is intimate, revealing his ability to tell deeply personal stories that resonate universally.

Cave's storytelling is also rooted in an exploration of faith, guilt, and redemption. His frequent biblical references and spiritual undertones give his narratives a mythic quality, elevating them beyond personal reflection into universal allegories. Whether he is writing about divine intervention, existential dread, or the fragility of love, his stories are imbued with a sense of urgency and significance.

Expanding Beyond Music: Novels and Screenwriting

Nick Cave's talents as a storyteller are not confined to music; he has also made significant contributions to literature and film. His ventures into these fields highlight his ability to craft compelling narratives beyond the structure of a song.

Novels: Gothic Prose and Existential Themes

Cave's debut novel, And the Ass Saw the Angel (1989), is a Southern Gothic masterpiece that showcases his ability to construct complex, atmospheric narratives. The novel follows Euchrid Eucrow, a mute outcast in a deeply religious community, and explores themes of alienation, divine punishment, and madness. The book's language is dense, lyrical, and often brutal, reflecting Cave's poetic tendencies. It stands as a literary extension of the themes he frequently explores in his music—religion, violence, and the search for meaning in suffering.

His second novel, The Death of Bunny Munro (2009), takes a different approach. It is a darkly comedic yet tragic tale of a sex-obsessed salesman spiraling into self-destruction following the death of his wife. Unlike his first novel, which is steeped in biblical and Gothic imagery, Bunny Munro is more contemporary, blending black humor with emotional depth. The novel reveals another facet of Cave's storytelling prowess—his ability to balance satire, pathos, and psychological complexity.

Screenwriting: Translating Stories to Film

Cave's storytelling skills have also extended into screenwriting. One of his most notable contributions is The Proposition (2005), a brutal Australian Western directed by John Hillcoat. The film, which follows a morally complex tale of lawlessness and justice, reflects Cave's penchant for mythic storytelling. The screenplay is poetic and raw, mirroring the stark, unforgiving landscapes of the Australian outback.

Cave also co-wrote Lawless (2012), a Prohibition-era crime drama starring Tom Hardy and Shia LaBeouf. Once again, his ability to craft morally ambiguous characters and intense, evocative dialogue is evident. His work in film demonstrates how seamlessly his narrative abilities translate across different artistic forms, reinforcing his reputation as a master storyteller.

Poetic Narratives and Rich Lyricism

At the heart of Cave's storytelling is his mastery of poetic language. His lyrics often resemble poetry in their structure, imagery, and rhythm. Whether he is describing a desolate landscape, a doomed romance, or a moment of divine revelation, his words carry a lyrical intensity that enhances the power of his storytelling.

Symbolism and Allegory

Cave frequently employs symbols and allegory to deepen his narratives. His songs are filled with religious imagery—crosses, angels, devils, and floods—which he uses to explore themes of sin, redemption, and human fallibility. In Red Right Hand, for example, the titular hand can be interpreted as a symbol of divine retribution, a sinister force, or unchecked power. The ambiguity of such symbols allows his stories to remain open to interpretation, adding layers of meaning for the listener.

His use of allegory is also evident in songs like The Weeping Song, which metaphorically explores grief and the inevitability of suffering. By embedding deeper meanings within his lyrics, Cave ensures that his songs function both as immediate emotional experiences and as thought-provoking works of art.

Evocative Imagery and Emotional Resonance

Cave's lyricism is often striking in its visual intensity. He paints scenes with words, immersing the listener in richly detailed landscapes—whether it's the dusty, lawless world of The Proposition, the feverish religious visions of And the Ass Saw the Angel, or the sorrowful reflections in The Boatman's Call. His ability to conjure vivid imagery makes his storytelling all the more powerful.

Beyond the visual elements, his lyrics also evoke deep emotional responses. Whether expressing raw grief in Ghosteen, the obsessive passion of Do You Love Me?, or the existential contemplation of Skeleton Tree, his words have an almost hypnotic effect. They resonate on both an intellectual and visceral level, drawing listeners into his world.

Cinematic and Literary Inspirations

Cave's storytelling is influenced by a range of cinematic and literary sources. His appreciation for film and literature is evident in the themes, structures, and stylistic choices of his work.

Literary Influences

Cave has drawn inspiration from literary giants such as William Faulkner, Flannery O'Connor, and Cormac McCarthy—writers known for their dense, atmospheric prose and exploration of moral ambiguity. Faulkner's influence, in particular, is evident in And the Ass Saw the Angel, with its

Southern Gothic setting and stream-of-consciousness narration.

His work also shows traces of Albert Camus and existential philosophy, particularly in his reflections on fate, death, and the absurdity of life. The characters in his songs and novels often struggle with existential dilemmas, questioning their place in a chaotic and indifferent world.

Cinematic Inspirations

Film has played a significant role in shaping Cave's narrative style. He has cited directors such as Werner Herzog, Terrence Malick, and David Lynch as influences, all of whom are known for their poetic and often surreal approach to storytelling. The dreamlike yet intense quality of Cave's lyrics echoes the atmosphere of Lynch's films, while the stark landscapes in The Proposition bear similarities to Malick's visual style.

Cave's own music videos often have a cinematic quality, with striking visuals that complement the narratives in his songs. His involvement in film scoring, particularly his collaborations with Warren Ellis on films like The Road and Hell or High Water, further cements his deep connection to cinematic storytelling.

Nick Cave's storytelling transcends the boundaries of music, literature, and film, making him one of the most dynamic and profound artists of his time. His ability to craft dark, poetic, and emotionally charged narratives has left an indelible mark on multiple artistic fields. Whether through haunting ballads, visceral novels, or gripping screenplays, Cave continues to push the boundaries of storytelling, proving that his creative vision knows no limits.

Chapter 9. The Red Hand Files: A Window Into His Thoughts

Nick Cave's artistic expression has always extended far beyond the music stage. His songwriting, novels, screenplays, and spoken-word performances have long served as outlets for his deep philosophical inquiries, reflections on grief, and ruminations on the human experience. However, perhaps the most intimate and direct connection Cave has cultivated with his audience comes through The Red Hand Files, an online platform where he personally responds to questions from fans, revealing profound insights into his mind, creative process, and worldview.

This project, launched in 2018, has become an evolving dialogue between Cave and his followers, offering a rare level of transparency from an artist often associated with mystique and enigma. The name itself is a reference to Red Right Hand, one of his most famous songs, reinforcing the idea of fate, morality, and the unknown forces that shape our lives—recurring themes in his body of work. Through The Red Hand Files, Cave strips away the barriers of celebrity and engages in deeply personal, sometimes raw conversations with those who seek his wisdom, offering a space where vulnerability and reflection take center stage.

Engaging with Fans Through Candid Reflections

Unlike traditional celebrity correspondence or the detached nature of social media interactions, The Red Hand Files functions as a deeply personal exchange. The questions fans send in range from the profound to the mundane, the tragic to the absurd. Cave, in turn, responds with a level of honesty, warmth, and philosophical introspection that feels almost confessional.

Some inquiries seek his thoughts on art, music, and literature. Others request advice on love, loss, and grief—topics that Cave is uniquely positioned to address, given his own experiences with personal tragedy. Many fans write to him about the deaths of loved ones, looking for solace in the words of someone who has grappled publicly with his own immense grief, particularly after the loss of his son Arthur in 2015.

Cave's responses are rarely straightforward. Instead, they are poetic, layered, and filled with a sense of wonder and curiosity. He does not offer easy answers but instead guides his readers toward deeper contemplation. His words are neither cynical nor indifferent, despite the darkness that pervades much of his music. Instead, they are brimming with empathy, an awareness of the human condition, and an insistence on finding meaning, however elusive, in pain and beauty alike.

In one particularly poignant response to a fan who lost a loved one, Cave wrote:

"Grief is not just the moment of loss, but the ongoing presence of an absence. It reshapes the world, colors every moment. Yet in grief, there is also transformation. Love does not die with the body; it lingers, finding new forms. The pain of loss is proof of loves endurance."

These words, like many of his responses, carry a poetic weight that transcends mere advice. They offer comfort, not by diminishing pain but by acknowledging it as an intrinsic part of the human experience.

Perspectives on Life, Art, and Human Experience

Through The Red Hand Files, Cave's perspectives on life, art, and the human condition have become an open book. He often discusses creativity as a mystical process, one that cannot be fully explained or controlled. He has spoken about the idea of songs "arriving" rather than being consciously crafted, describing songwriting as an act of discovery rather than pure invention.

One particularly revealing moment came when a fan asked how he continues to write after suffering profound personal loss. Cave's response was both devastating and enlightening:

"After Arthur died, I felt as though all my words had left me. There was a great silence, an emptiness where language used to be. But slowly, painfully, the words returned—not as they were before, but changed, imbued with a different kind of weight. I write now not to escape grief, but to make sense of it, to keep moving forward, to keep Arthur close."

This perspective reveals the evolution of his relationship with art—not as a separate entity from his personal struggles, but as something inseparable from them. His work, especially recent albums like Ghosteen, has reflected this transformation, embracing a more ethereal, meditative tone.

Cave's thoughts on human relationships are equally insightful. He has spoken about love as an act of surrender, of allowing oneself to be vulnerable in a world where nothing is guaranteed. In discussing his marriage to Susie Bick, he often refers to love as a stabilizing force, something that anchors him amid chaos.

On the topic of faith, Cave's views are complex and ever-evolving. While biblical imagery has permeated his lyrics for decades, he does not align himself strictly with any religious doctrine. Instead, he speaks of belief as a fluid, shifting force—something that both haunts and inspires him. He has written about prayer, not as an act of devotion to a particular deity, but as a way of articulating longing, hope, and gratitude.

"To pray is to acknowledge the vastness of the unknown, to reach toward something greater than ourselves, even if we are uncertain of what it is."

Cave's ability to articulate the intangible—to put words to emotions and experiences that often feel beyond language—is what makes The Red Hand Files such a compelling space. It is not merely a Q&A platform; it is an ongoing philosophical discourse, a space where art and life converge in profound and unexpected ways.

The Evolution of an Artist Through Direct Dialogue

Throughout his career, Nick Cave has embodied many personas—the preacher, the storyteller, the rock star, the poet. But through The Red Hand Files, he presents himself as something even more radical: a human being willing to be seen in all his complexity.

This project is not just a way for him to connect with fans; it is a form of art in itself. His responses are carefully crafted, infused with a sense of literary beauty that makes them feel like extensions of his songwriting. The difference is that here, the interaction is immediate and intimate. There is no stage, no music to carry the message—just words, raw and direct.

Over time, The Red Hand Files has taken on a life of its own. It has become a sanctuary for those seeking understanding, a place where people can ask their deepest questions and receive answers that are thoughtful, poetic, and unflinchingly honest. Cave does not claim to have all the answers, but he offers something just as valuable: the willingness to engage, to listen, to reflect.

In an era where many artists maintain a carefully curated distance from their audiences, Cave's approach is refreshingly different. He does not filter his emotions or attempt to maintain a flawless image. Instead, he embraces uncertainty, contradiction, and imperfection—qualities that have always defined his music and now define his written reflections as well.

As The Red Hand Files continues to grow, so does its impact. It is not just a repository of Cave's thoughts but a living document of his evolution as an artist and as a person. Through this ongoing dialogue, he reaffirms the power of language to heal, to connect, and to illuminate the darkest corners of human experience.

Nick Cave has always been a storyteller, but with The Red Hand Files, he has become something even more profound: a witness to the lives of others, a guide through the labyrinth of love, loss, and longing. And in doing so, he has shown that art is not just something we consume—it is something that binds us together, that makes sense of the chaos, that reminds us we are not alone.

Chapter 10. Cultural Impact and Legacy

Nick Cave's artistic reach extends far beyond music, cementing his status as a creative force whose work resonates across rock, literature, and the arts. His ability to craft deeply evocative narratives, whether through his music, novels, or film contributions, has positioned him as one of the most distinctive and influential figures in contemporary culture.

Impact on Rock and Alternative Music

Cave's influence on rock music is vast and multifaceted. From his early days with The Birthday Party to his decades-long career with Nick Cave & The Bad Seeds, he has continually redefined the boundaries of post-punk, gothic rock, and alternative music. His willingness to explore dark, complex themes—love, death, violence, and redemption—has inspired countless musicians.

The Birthday Party's aggressive and chaotic sound laid the groundwork for noise rock and post-punk movements, influencing artists such as The Jesus and Mary Chain and Swans. With The Bad Seeds,

Cave refined his approach, blending elements of blues, jazz, gospel, and folk into a sound that was both haunting and cinematic. Albums like Murder Ballads and The Boatman's Call showcased his storytelling prowess, drawing admiration from musicians across genres, from alternative rock to folk and even metal.

Bands such as Arctic Monkeys, PJ Harvey, and Mark Lanegan have cited Cave as a major influence, admiring his ability to weave literary narratives into his music. His duets, particularly his collaborations with Kylie Minogue on Where the Wild Roses Grow and PJ Harvey on Henry Lee, illustrate his range and ability to create strikingly emotional performances.

His impact extends to film soundtracks as well, with collaborations on movies like The Assassination of Jesse James by the Coward Robert Ford and The Proposition (which he also wrote). His atmospheric compositions, often alongside Warren Ellis, have redefined the way music shapes cinematic storytelling, influencing modern film scores.

Influence on Literature

Beyond music, Cave has made an indelible mark on literature. His lyrical style, characterized by poetic depth and biblical allusions, has often been compared to the works of Leonard Cohen and Bob Dylan. However, Cave's literary ambitions extend further, with novels such as And the Ass Saw the Angel and The Death of Bunny Munro showcasing his ability to craft rich, immersive narratives.

And the Ass Saw the Angel (1989) reflects Cave's Southern Gothic influences, drawing inspiration from William Faulkner and Flannery O'Connor. The novel's dense, lyrical prose mirrors the dark, surreal landscapes found in his music. The Death of Bunny Munro (2009), a more contemporary and psychologically driven narrative, explores themes of masculinity, desire, and self-destruction, reflecting his continued interest in deeply flawed characters.

Cave's literary presence is also felt in his Red Hand Files, an ongoing collection of deeply personal letters responding to fans questions. These writings have further solidified his reputation as an intellectual and philosophical artist, willing to engage in profound discussions on grief, love, and the human condition. His reflections, particularly in the wake of personal tragedy, have resonated with a broad audience, extending his influence into philosophical and self-reflective discourse.

Impact on Film, Theater, and Visual Arts

Cave's contributions to cinema go beyond scoring films. His work as a screenwriter, particularly in collaboration with director John Hillcoat, has produced critically acclaimed films like The Proposition (2005) and Lawless (2012). His ability to craft raw, poetic scripts filled with moral ambiguity has influenced modern screenwriting, particularly in the realm of revisionist Westerns and crime dramas.

His impact on visual arts is equally significant. His striking image—often dressed in dark, tailored suits with an almost mythic presence—has made him a subject of fascination for photographers and visual artists. His performances, particularly in recent years, have taken on an almost theatrical quality, with an emphasis on intimacy and audience engagement.

In 2023, the documentary This Much I Know to Be True captured Cave's artistic process, revealing the interplay between music, visual storytelling, and existential reflection. The film further cemented his reputation as a multifaceted artist whose work transcends mediums.

Enduring Relevance and Evolution Over Time

One of the most remarkable aspects of Nick Cave's career is his ability to remain relevant while continually evolving as an artist. Unlike many musicians who fade into nostalgia, Cave has consistently pushed boundaries, adapting his sound and artistic approach to new eras while maintaining his core identity.

From Punk Provocateur to Poetic Storyteller

Cave's early career with The Birthday Party was defined by chaos, raw energy, and rebellion. The band's music, steeped in nihilism and punk aggression, captured the disillusionment of the post-punk era. However, as he transitioned to The Bad Seeds, Cave began refining his artistic approach, embracing a more narrative-driven and musically diverse style.

This shift was evident in albums like The Firstborn Is Dead (1985), which explored blues influences, and Your Funeral... My Trial (1986), which demonstrated a growing maturity in storytelling.

The Good Son (1990) marked a further transformation, incorporating orchestral arrangements and deeply introspective lyrics.

The Balladeer of Loss and Longing

Cave's ability to evolve became even more apparent in the late 1990s with The Boatman's Call (1997). This album, a departure from his previous dark and violent narratives, was deeply personal, reflecting on love, heartbreak, and spirituality. It showcased Cave's ability to strip down his sound to its emotional core, paving the way for a new phase in his career.

As he entered the 2000s, Cave continued to reinvent himself. No More Shall We Part (2001) and Abattoir Blues/The Lyre of Orpheus (2004) combined his literary depth with grand, expansive instrumentation. At the same time, he embraced more spontaneous, raw energy with his side project, Grinderman, which harkened back to his punk roots.

Navigating Grief and Finding New Meaning

Cave's later work, particularly following the tragic death of his son Arthur in 2015, has been defined by profound grief and transformation. Skeleton

Tree (2016) and Ghosteen (2019) marked a stark departure from his previous works, embracing ambient soundscapes, meditative lyricism, and a deeply personal exploration of loss. These albums resonated widely, touching listeners who had experienced personal tragedy and further elevating Cave as an artist capable of profound emotional connection.

His live performances also evolved in this period. Once known for his dark, intense stage presence, Cave began engaging more directly with audiences, fostering an almost spiritual communion during concerts. His 2020 Conversations with Nick Cave tour, where he answered audience questions in an intimate setting, demonstrated his commitment to dialogue and connection.

A Legacy That Continues to Grow

Nick Cave's influence shows no signs of waning. His recent works, including collaborations with Warren Ellis and the continuation of The Red Hand Files, reflect an artist who is still deeply engaged with the world and his audience. Unlike many artists who stagnate, Cave continues to challenge himself, embracing new artistic directions and philosophical inquiries.

His legacy is one of transformation—of a musician, writer, and artist who has continually evolved while staying true to his artistic essence. From the anarchic energy of The Birthday Party to the profound meditations of Ghosteen, Cave's journey is one of relentless creativity, intellectual depth, and emotional resonance.

As his influence extends to new generations of musicians, writers, and artists, Nick Cave remains a singular figure in cultural history—a storyteller whose work, like the myths and legends he often draws upon, will endure long after his voice has faded.

11. Conclusion

Nick Cave's artistic journey is a testament to the power of reinvention, raw emotional depth, and an unwavering commitment to storytelling. Over the decades, he has established himself as not just a musician, but a poet, novelist, and cultural icon whose work transcends generations. His songs and writings explore the darkest corners of human existence while also illuminating moments of grace, love, and redemption. From the visceral intensity of his early punk-infused days with The Birthday Party to the haunting beauty of Ghosteen, Cave's evolution as an artist has been marked by a profound engagement with themes that remain timeless.

As his career continues to inspire, Cave's enduring impact is rooted in his ability to explore fundamental aspects of the human condition—love and loss, faith and doubt, violence and beauty. His work does not offer easy answers but instead compels audiences to confront the contradictions and complexities of existence. Whether through his gripping narratives, his evocative use of biblical imagery, or his deeply personal reflections on grief,

Cave has built a body of work that remains as compelling as ever.

The Power of Storytelling

At the heart of Nick Cave's artistry is his unparalleled ability to tell stories. His songs unfold like cinematic vignettes, filled with striking characters, dramatic landscapes, and an acute sense of tension. Albums such as Murder Ballads exemplify his mastery of dark, gothic storytelling, where love and death are intertwined in ways both poetic and brutal. This storytelling extends beyond music—his novels, including And the Ass Saw the Angel and The Death of Bunny Munro, showcase a similarly unflinching exploration of obsession, depravity, and redemption.

Cave's gift as a storyteller lies in his ability to tap into deep archetypes and mythologies. His narratives often feel timeless, drawing on biblical allegories, folklore, and literary influences ranging from William Faulkner to Leonard Cohen. His characters are haunted figures—murderers, lovers, drifters—caught in existential struggles that mirror our own search for meaning. This relentless pursuit of truth, no matter how painful or unsettling, gives his work a timeless resonance.

The Duality of Darkness and Light

Few artists embrace the duality of human nature as completely as Nick Cave. His music is often described as dark, but this darkness is never without purpose. Cave's work does not dwell in misery for the sake of it; instead, it seeks to understand suffering, violence, and loss in the broader context of love, redemption, and hope.

This contrast is particularly evident in albums like The Boatman's Call and Ghosteen, where moments of deep sorrow are counterbalanced by a yearning for beauty and transcendence. The latter, written in the wake of his son's tragic death, is a meditation on grief that avoids easy catharsis, instead offering a deeply spiritual reflection on loss and transformation. This ability to juxtapose despair with moments of profound beauty is what makes Cave's music so emotionally powerful.

Moreover, Cave's lyrics frequently wrestle with religious imagery and questions of faith. He has never positioned himself as a believer in the traditional sense, yet his work is steeped in biblical references, parables, and moral dilemmas that suggest a deep spiritual engagement. Whether he is invoking the wrath of God or searching for divine grace, Cave's music captures the push and pull between doubt and belief, between sin and redemption.

Reinvention and Evolution

One of the most remarkable aspects of Cave's career is his capacity for reinvention. While many artists remain confined to a particular sound or aesthetic, Cave has constantly pushed himself into new creative territories. From the punk aggression of The Birthday Party to the gothic blues of early Bad Seeds albums, and from the stripped-back intimacy of The Boatman's Call to the atmospheric landscapes of Push the Sky Away, each phase of his career has revealed new depths to his artistry.

This willingness to evolve has kept his work relevant across generations. Younger artists continue to cite him as an influence, and his collaborations with musicians from Kylie Minogue to Warren Ellis demonstrate his openness to new sounds and ideas. The transition from the raw, literary narratives of Murder Ballads to the ethereal, meditative quality of Ghosteen is a testament to his refusal to become stagnant.

Even beyond music, Cave's ventures into literature, film, and screenwriting highlight his expansive artistic vision. His novel The Death of Bunny Munro explores themes of obsession and downfall with the same intensity as his songs, while his work in screenwriting (The Proposition, Lawless) showcases his ability to craft atmospheric, morally complex narratives in film.

An Artist in Conversation with His Audience

Unlike many enigmatic artists who remain distant from their audience, Cave has fostered an intimate and ongoing dialogue with his fans. His Red Hand Files—a platform where he personally responds to fan questions—has become an extension of his artistry, revealing his insights on grief, creativity, love, and the nature of art itself.

Through this direct engagement, Cave has cultivated a unique relationship with his listeners. He does not present himself as an untouchable figure but rather as someone willing to share his own struggles and vulnerabilities. This transparency has only deepened the connection between his work and his audience, making his music feel even more personal and immediate.

Legacy and Influence

Nick Cave's impact extends far beyond his own discography. His work has shaped the landscape of alternative music, inspiring artists across multiple genres. Figures like PJ Harvey, Mark Lanegan, and even contemporary indie and rock musicians have drawn from his raw lyricism and atmospheric storytelling.

His influence is not limited to music—his literary contributions and film work have also left an indelible mark on modern storytelling. His ability to craft evocative narratives has made him a touchstone for writers and filmmakers who seek to blend poetry with grit, beauty with brutality.

But perhaps Cave's greatest legacy is the emotional depth he brings to his work. In an era where much of popular music leans toward surface-level themes, his ability to explore the profound complexities of life, death, and love ensures that his music remains deeply resonant. Whether through the apocalyptic fury of Tupelo, the fragile beauty of Into My Arms, or the ghostly reflections of Bright Horses, his songs continue to speak to the human experience in ways that few others can.

Conclusion

Nick Cave's career is one of unrelenting artistic exploration. His music, writing, and storytelling have cemented him as one of the most compelling artists of his generation. Through his ability to weave intricate narratives, his willingness to explore life's most profound questions, and his refusal to remain creatively static, he has crafted a body of work that remains timeless.

His themes—love and loss, faith and doubt, violence and redemption—are universal, ensuring that his art will continue to resonate with future generations. Whether through the brooding intensity of Murder Ballads or the spectral beauty of Ghosteen, Cave's work offers a reflection of the human soul in all its complexity.

As he continues to evolve, one thing remains clear: Nick Cave is not just a musician, but a storyteller, a poet, and an artist whose influence will endure long after the last note has faded. His ability to capture both the darkness and the light of existence ensures that his legacy will remain as haunting and beautiful as the music he has created.

Printed in Great Britain
by Amazon